Dummy Fire

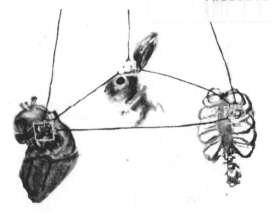

Sarah Vap

Winner of the 2006 Saturnalia Books Poetry Contest
Selected by Forrest Gander

saturnalia books

Saturnalia Books
13 E. Highland Ave.
2nd Floor
Philadelphia, PA 19118
info @ www.saturnaliabooks.com

ISBN 978-0-9754990-5-4

Book Design by Saturnalia Books
Printing by Westcan Printing Group, Canada.

Cover Ar by Bruno Sipavicius
Copyright 2007 © Bruno Sipivicius

Author Photograph: Todd Fredson

Distributed by:
Small Press Distribution
1341 Seventh Street
Berkeley, CA 94710-1409
1-800-869-7553

With deep gratitude for my teachers Norman Dubie, Beckian Fritz Goldberg, Jeannine Savard, and Cynthia Hogue, for their help with these poems.

Thank you to Arizona State University's Creative Writing Program, and Karla Elling, for giving me the time and the support needed to write this book.

Respect and gratitude to Europos Parkas in Vilnius, Lithuania.

Joyful thanks to my friends and fellow poets for their insight and assistance with these poems.

Grateful acknowledgement to the editors of the following publications in which these poems first appeared: *42 Opus, Barrow Street, Dragonfire, Diner, Field, EM Literary, The Fiddlehead, Gentle Strength Review, Literatura ir Menas, Poezijos Pavasaris, Rainbow Curve, SHADE,* and *Skein.*

for Todd

Contents

You who have loved me
    for my little beginning
        of love for you.

                            – Rilke

The soul inaugurates.

                            – Bachelard

Everything Offered Happens

I suspect there are two things
going on here: a cry-accident, and the patience that built you.

I don't believe in geological time—so no one can tell me
when to begin. Vapor remains here, behind the circulating

heavy station, increasingly simpler. I love that whole idea.
The idea we hold over ourselves, especially sitting

near the bed. Especially in one ear. I love the idea
that it feels good to be here, without apology

for how good you are. I wish
I had been nicer; I laugh for things. Love

their approximations. This is as close as I can get:

everything must be loved—omens wait
in the deep-freeze, rocking at night. I'm a little embarrassed

by what I love. Intimate with thousands. More and more
I wish it wasn't so hard for you.

That it hadn't been made so hard. I wish angels would come
with wings of cedar. I've invited one,

especially, to sleep near me. To signal, and to include
the exact time.

kansas, my birth.

a beetle's
too technical for nature, which prefers

slowly; so matte

it's undetectable. someday i'll be able to say i've kept
and given away.

that i've wished to keep
every child—but cede, poignantly, until

death-wish comes to check.   baskets, jugs, a rhubarb
tang—glorifying

repentance, and after
repentance the marbled grasses, genetic memory.

it's why my grandfather's cornfields frighten—maniacal
seeding; *vigilance* that i long for.

and your indulgence,   —accepting

that i *do* exist, on faith, until
i'm harmless. no— grass, soil, grass. until
inconsequential.

Sister Sleepwalks in Kona

Bees at the beach shower. Five maidens in succession panting like oxen. Her wrists are like goats in a stall.

She tells Bonnie that the ocean comes from the shower, bullets like bees from yellow canaries. The goat comes from the wrists and the maidens from scattered hair.

She doesn't know how to stop. No little canary. Imaginary, like memory. Like inventing a loved person. She wears the coconut palms;

Clyde, a housedress and panama hat. Shells in pockets and a mango sapling by the speckled horse.
She sterilizes the bird on a flame.

Rinses her dress and puts it on wet—lavender waves.

The divining shells say something about New Zealand. How it's always against you

and the whole Human Adventure— sitting with its suitcase by the door.
Something about pentimento, and moving from brightness

toward trust. She remembers a horse tied up in the night, walks toward mother who wears the yellow dress of canaries.

A green scarf and her drink. Hay on pavement, and mother's nose bleeds into tomato soup.   My sister says we could ask for less.

Could always lure a cat. Ten cats
the afternoon she lay down in a pineapple field.

Crackers fall from mother's mouth into the soup. Sister says let's steal a goat,
and raise it. All her fallen hair, into the pocket of the traveler's saddle.

She says we go at night.

She says Sister, honey, my thunderbird. With the little, actual eyes of the thunderbird.

Who knows how long this way

Her body's customs,

he requires that she shave
not like a girl.

His passing imagines her own,

it's nothing, though—

she just climbs out of the forest,
forearms swollen from horseflies.

Her eyes swollen— and smears him
on her body not knowing

how she intends

to live. So shows
him something— pollen,

a powerful arm, and vodka
souring his balls.

Nothing left but oldness,
she shifts his skin

like a lover. With all this knowledge

of her, he really
had nothing to choose.

Nightmare

I would live and die with them.
Jade hooves,

light-blue teeth and lions
in their manes. They've missed

the chance to get
this life the way they wanted it.

Always hidden
or kicking the maid to death

who went by, thrashing a little. Raped,
thrown into burning lime.

But they've charmed again. Shown me
the good, beautiful cages
in the fog. I should

have more to remember.
I can only say that I waited,

and they came.

Land of Blue Snow: A Christmas Poem

The edge
of the lake like a thread

blown
slowly forward.

Song about a rider gathering early waves
from broken water—

Prophet and his reindeer. His fingerprints
on black glass. The animals turn,
teeth to hindquarter,

while we tell him things.

Bandages of rain on branches trick us.
Reindeer moss tricks us. No one

has to agree with me. You might think
of something to praise,

to not remember. You remember
quiet, and slowly. The pilgrimage,

his girls. Reconcile: eight hot hells
and eight cold hells. The lake

will not freeze
until it swallows autumn's head:

this one wears a white dress.
In the diamond-grove—so few colors,

even the color on edge. Turquoise flower
which doesn't understand you, yaws

fatally apart. Search, smell—this giant of ice
that makes winter sexual.

do it the way god does it

the woman he is with, her legs
move evermore slowly.

she has borne
in secret the want

that opens true things
at little angles.

it wasn't important—

Fisherman's Christmas

Hermit on the peninsula surrounded
by air, and eleven red snapdragons. His dog costs

a light-brown penny where dog-tooth violets
grow. Lavender, moral animals.

Dog-enthusiasms which let you
count, really count. Calm winter

kills the bright winter star. His daybreak dream
of having, of growing on the throat

over and over. Of cocktail knuckles
and a girl who exposes herself. A girl

who throws bread at the neighbor's dog. Loaves,
like little songs

of daughters in the wading pool. Like throwing fingers.
Like throwing tigers. The paid-for tigers.

Paper tigers, paper snowflakes
– for T.F.

and thirst in the form of a bird.
Watchful

myrtle, with myrtle-birds calculating the red knots
in fresh oranges. The spiritists and fish

are snatched by crows. By a cat
with its whiskers in a hut. Hut

in a forest that comforts him; that caught
him watching from the top of wolf-tree

across the snow—— *foxes becoming orange*.

Birds for weeks on oily wings, like that red-faced insect
in the bite of bread and tea.

Like the flat snake, it has to do with being blessed.
The wolf-tree is made of lead, and of paper.

Paper thorns all around the coming-back-baby.
The fish-farm. And yes, around baby.

Babies that scent our throats. Throats the color
of the lion's eyes. Guess it, apologists

to measure donkey-knockers
on cranes, and the plutonium-basket.

Measure enough tea to make spit. The neck
is caped, as they say. A neck, and curious.

Eventide

Unbearable dress—do you have a secret
memory of a cow

tormented by the gadfly. *What the fuck is the gadfly?*

Unaccountable—why there's a planetarium in the Nebraska
cornfield. Io is the closest
of Jupiter's moons. Galileo

found the cashcow first. Tart. Flippant. Cowgirl-magnificat
in the vulnerable dress.

Crackpot

There's less time, nestled   you know
how water narrows or people throw up their hands

and say *this can't be right.*   Where debt predicts
receiving—   where something is both tiny and heavy
we want something that never

breaks down. Why would that world behave the same way
as the one big and light? What we feel as force

is message. A primitive so technical
as to be written in gloriole.

crying into the rushlight and candlelight of winter—
how blake was born.

the angel at my birth, with the plainest whitish
patina. her gloves… nightcap bent downward

and studying me. workmanlike visions—declining westward

to star-child, or changeling—the new genealogy:
a tabula rasa. carte

blanche. a *bona-*

fide who despised landscapes and women… bland
and mutual neglects.   despite something

about our first parents— that very
personal enormity which peeps, then runs to seed.

as if compromised by any tie—i didn't mean

to do this my whole life.

Poem translated loosely from the Lithuanian

like ticks crawling

something sky,
a sky which is different

pity, oh!

the midnight tree, oh grass

if you haven't,
if I have nothing else—

rain on the windshield
moves with the trees,

the tips,

his smell like sawing the wood
of olive. a certain

rain, more like—

good,
it's already over

Christmas Morning: Dying the Saint's Beard

1.
Going to the body

who is going to the lake. Conclusions,
like a daybreak train. A feathered headdress,

hard yellow at the tips of his fingers.

Holes he dug
for playing marbles, and the gift-ring—

a long story he has told. Cupping his genitals
in sleep, dreams of eating esophagus.

2.
Of the gigantic mechanical horse

that gallops around his father's river.
His father's wild dance:

duplicate braids from his chin.
Night insects, day insects

long and soft with algae. The night-leaf
is his invoice.

The Built-In Accident
– A Marriage of Heaven and Earth

Every time you think you're done, you're not—it's the moment
you choose to go back to. It's the meaning of romance, beforehand. Memory

thaws tiny flames out of cans. Daybreak from the bottom of the pit.
It surfaces fish in strict winter.

Sly gamekillers, you are guided by the Supper Star. Carried off, twirling.
(You must be very vigilant, or you'll be taken away.)

That dog wouldn't budge from your heels, you have to understand
how humbling it was. Fetal circumstance,

mute place, triangulation. The contracts of incest. Back then,
people marry people they don't love.

Conscience, I suppose, needs thinning. Has imagined
much: land-owner, pig, born-again—a kind of hanging.

A kind of task, I call it *morning*.

Such Sunlight

So languidly

he got up from it, like smoke—
the most he dared.

I tickle the boy's back
until he sleeps.

Whisper
his fingers into mine—

bags of children,
the three kings asleep.

What the greedy sun will do next

Ear to ear
with the young man too young for me,

terribly sorry and that helps.

Beautiful unusual dress—clouds
warm themselves

and all they will eat are diamonds
from the pineapples. Sun's

great over-steppings,

mornings when I am most full of you,
most foreign to myself.

When I can't
recognize water. It's too hard

for us to ease. Tactful,

wild animals at the edge of the forest
help

the sun roll back
into darkness and hang

the dress that helps.

Birthright

A deck of cards on the corner. The sun led steadily away; no better
for it. Sitting around in paper gowns, in deep study. The colors fall
out of their hair. The road that stopped coming. All of their beauti-
ful moves. Listen, there's nothing else to do. The dog's bruised eye.

The Two of Us At One O'clock

We hardly ever shower anymore. I make you kneel on rice. You
wrestle, biting my hand and throwing i-ching all at once.
Somewhere it is raining. Here, just cool. And let me not love you,
you say. And let you not.

A clock dangles, and the stillness—somewhere far away what is
wanted: the bat's frog. A cave of three hands together. The rich
man's crimson portals.

Under the Window, a Square of Light

1.
A brother piled and coiled
in calm rice water,

a brother in bed, or in baths
showing you the brown half

of his beard. A body becoming
joy,

imagined only as joy.
If you see him

in the necks of trees,
hands the shape of palms,

mouths like brother's
feet leaving.
Brother whose features—

water moving
over legs, icelight that snaps

in the ears. Ice in the eyes.
If you see him in the shaved

field of safe cows, pull stones
over him. Pull him

into the half-full bed. Kneel
and break

the ice from his water.

2.
The stone blanket sways.
My brother's light hair,

dead legs, legs
of a killed thing, follow

his ear to the floor of the sea.
My foot on the water I feel

the moon, the funny brother,
the tiger pillow folding over itself

beneath him; remember
looking at the lake he says

it's so still the fish must not breathe—
the fish with strings of light that are their shit.

3.
I believe everything,
he says, I am here.

When I think of him:

He and his dogs come out
of water. He's covered

with dogs, with water.
Each time, a woman calls.

I tell him I am the man, I show
him the trees, I show him his sisters.

I give him the man
bound together with wires.

He wants nothing
to return. He strains to hear

his man of stars, the gold
of a waiting brother,

sunlight resting,
if you believe that.

Cure Chair

Break upward, infant year. Naked
without its ending. The beginning

of the war is never secret.

Benches. Two birds in bush. Gadfly,
secrecy's not a belief

of mine. Another, more particular,
bird in hand. The birds are completely unable

to reassure. Bums, by the river, reassure.
Hard-on dolls from Romania and Latvian

sketches of stallions reassure. Father's

testicles—sitting and throwing
i-ching, that's all there is to tell.

To do: ride herd. The shifty talk of oracles—
tell me only

if it doesn't hurt to tell. Wishfully,
I agree. To a tryst. With a star about

to nova. A star that will calm down, and help
the things that die. Bright crabs

hunt ticks. Ruined
and ruining world.

X times X is X

We love antibiotics, a rash
    like a lover's across the chest.

Weights on her legs, moons touch

themselves. The moon
    falls through the sky,

does it help,
        Moon? Sod to her thighs—
        shit-black.

The romance hospital is dull.
        Yellowish cancers on her face,
        cancers that smell

to her dog. Her head is bouncing
        the moonlightway...

she thinks her underpants are two kittens
        without lungs. Without the Inca's zero
        or the two princesses

asleep inside the pomegranate;
        the pomegranate tree

where stray kittens play.
        We think her gown

should be human
        behind that zodiacal door.

Essay on Skinning a Fox

The great blue heron killed
in the storm to our kitchen table.
Cut the wings, blue

on blue on blue

from the body and the head
from the neck. Her beak, bright

yellow-orange. Wings spread

on the board to dry. Or as,
at last, lights entering the city

where swans
run to the Flathead.

Do you want to kill this fish?
You say Finn MacCool

ate his Salmon of Wisdom
and I will kill

this fish. *Touching gills
is always fatal.* I ease my hands
under the fish's belly

until I've cradled beneath her head,
a lover might. A fox
on the road at night. Hesitates, then runs

with its broken leg.

Burning the Tick off the Snake

He dragged it out by the tail saying *Jesus loves you*,
then began to burn the lump on her side.

Seconds later it rained

into the smoke while grass burned
and deer jumped rock banks to the river. He said *Confess*

and the tick lost its hold. The forest floor turned black,
the town smelled for days under pelvis-shaped clouds—

neon from the fires. Flowers melted to the field
and mammoth clumps of trees hulked,

senseless. He said *Repent* while onlookers gave mouth to mouth
to the cat-sized fawn and the hill flapped like an orange tarp.

The windmill's arms caught what water they could,
and cattle died cooling themselves in belly-deep trenches of mud.

Spring Ranch, Nebraska

1.

We find his hair in dried paint, then plant cattails to hide the corn from her kitchen window. Inhaling and spitting out gnats she says that by the end he couldn't swallow, choked on spit. And shows me the automatic writings of the woman who communicates with grandfather two farms down. He says *planet earth*. Advises grandmother on the weather, on the harvest. Then she melts silver with a battery into boiled water. Bottles it, and gives it to me for mouthwash.

2.

Pink bee-bush, rose mallow, and wild grapes. Stinking water in the tornado shelter and the sod house full of buffalo robes. Beyond the firebreak, ice still covers the horse pond. Three children and the leftover duck share a quilt while she stitches true-lovers knots on the saddle.

3.

Grandfather puts his cigarette in the horse's mouth for a joke, says he once broke sod with oxen. Says it isn't the air that is blue, that the grass was a shade he can't describe. We know smartweed, bluestem, and buffalo grass. We know where the man threshed his son, where red grass was last plowed under, and where red dust lay the deepest.

4.

One amber glass in winter for color. She stuffs the bed with dried
russian thistle and paper, imagines the snow as *chinese white*. Like
prairie dogs they've gone underground for winter. The plaster laid
on the earthen walls tastes sweet to the children. They pull horse-
hair from the mixture of clay, blood, and lime when she goes out-
side for the milk that is cooling on the snow.

What you've taught me—

my mother and father lusting
to make me again. Dead grandfather

approves. Speaks to me

more than ever about
leaving myself. About

being wrapped
together, wrappings

—the lap
of a child. The turquoise

doors to our house. They think
we're lovers and wonder
what we need

or hold. Your father's
bees, the hive

on fire, the honey also
on fire and the bees

spark. I understood something.
What you are trying

to do and when.
You come to me, but why.

more you never get to know

the most interior:

entered into
another person's hand,

too intimate—

black sheets of water

below a naked light
and the ammonia of the semen

unlearned by learning
someone else's sounds

and that's all.

warming and calming
and talk talk talk.

Conception of Thief-Horse *(I am Thief-Horse)*

A house that unfolds

underwater, it has been genealogical so long.
Behind the bed, five imaginary objects: vague dormer.

Deadlight. Gelding,
because he will never undress. Because

he didn't let her into his room. Hay and tar cottage
by the stone dike, listening.

I think of him as late. I think
he probably felt he had nothing to lose.

Fish-wife, whose eggs taste
of fish. Every horse has to be born—

or the water will stay and stay. If my parents
lived longer, his boots would be treated

with train-oil—they'd do the little
things for each other. And within their work

is my need: horse like a boulder

into the current, with studious

words of return. It's the old story—living
child takes the dead child. Takes fish-wife.

Takes the gelding and confuses *horse*
with *house*. The child turns into water,

less swimming. Truly, no one
came or was caused to come.

On Trading Strings For Clefts

Salt film on the neck. Sitting alone in the flowers that make you classy. We never thought you were that bright—a girl who will be thrown from a car. Who will be quiet for the money. Amazed that such a cow was willing to be touched, everything messy. We know you see something beautiful. That you are paid to fold something, fold something: red clay beneath the cherry tree, and hail that spares the cherries. The dress you buried in sand; this water, this ripple-line; the gauze gown and the sky. Bright clouds are the scooped-out firepond. Udders swing in the brine.

Earth's Second-Skin

— after Levertov

Glassware   and earthenware—
the earth's best beard,

its schizophrenic aspects.
        Woman, in the shape of a woman,

measures the depth of snow
with a pole. Steam above the snow. A couple more poles—

then earth's mundane refusal.
                She's really forgotten

why she's here.   All the possibilities
at the close weren't there. Count it

toward her survival: one wreck weathered,

        one might be left—on the floor,
        in the whale. In terms of sacrifice,

the light pours out of her, very common.
Practicing kindness—
        she can pull, in repose,

distinct glass feathers, or
a brazil nut from the heart's margin. In the range

of open time, she cannot see
the beloved who rides with her.

A good head on my shoulders.

Sunday paper: youngsters with petroleum
jelly—to speed-up pink hula hoops,   something to cure the hysteria.
Lock of hair,

head of hair smelling like the tuberose and triumphant
entry.   Anoint his head or his feet. Waste either

love or perfume. Indulgences owe
their potency to famous amounts: three hundred pence.

Thirty pieces of silver.   Pound
of flesh and the multitudes.

Midnight's Prism

Tiny paintings on stems, they quiet
then double.

At midnight by raindrop
and wind. They quiet,

then double. Fur of grass,
on black—alphabets of stars.
On death, stars breathe in

then crack
messages in the wind

we'll ignore.

The house
waits for us, its blue smoke

and crystal of salt.

We quiet,
then couple.

Thicket of little fish—
what I could find in the ice.

Gold, arranged: we cut—

they double, then
they double.

The night finds hard to find

For midday it is easy—wind

knocks the smell of lilac
into your shirt. Into your small storm

like lace. Snails clog the drain, and the mirrors
and the orchard do not break; but an end

for each. The children
escape with a share of oil and fire. With the key
in the water. A statement

of number and the mosquitoes

mumble—

Thinned by fire, the groves—

the sisters have not walked; are entered.
She thinks, even at night, the way they rise, soft, lit—
without having to push. Or,

agree on much except
against the branches.

How long winter, that won't bend. Won't harden
or wither if, where father cursed

the snow and sidestepped
charred hills. Never bows. Mother grows old

rubbing rose-quartz; an ease
will soon be gone. The mountain

will hide whatever hoped to burn there.

If she'd removed her boots as little sister prefers
she'd know the ground,

these hills without firelines—
she shouldn't be inside.

Rests at dawn, the grove: half-black. Half-green. The ridge

would show her the vultures. She belongs

with either sister. Hiking down, imagines
amethyst deer in the trees.

Body on the Mountain

Several hundred miles of tulips. The fetlock sunk into mud. Doing what we don't need to know about to the steel spines of the violets. To the dog's nipples hanging just off the dirt. To the jade chimes, stone chimes, water clock. Burned air. To your back-dimples and man-breasts. To the limping dog, the painted dog, the just-walking-away-dog. A dog like your father's. A dog rubbed and fuchsia. It's just like you, dangling a whip because you can't be the countess. It's just like you to give four bad horses to a dying woman.

Snippets, overheard at his wedding

I.
enormous tits
(the taste of his mother still in his mouth)

one of my great-grand-somethings died of gangrene,
another climbed and climbed until he dissolved.
They both had pepperhair and whippings

the impulse is not to distinguish,
but to link—
like steam trains to Cairo fueled by mummies;
like cures for impotence made with a ground-up mummy

at the dinner hour all things move,
even the Moravian virgins—don't be too beautiful

and they ground their grandfather's bones into the beer.
The powder, like the white film on old chocolate,
did not affect the taste

Following the recipe of Herodotus they pounded the nail
into the nostrils, used a bronze wire to scramble the brain,
then removed it by turning the corpse upside down and pouring
out the nose

with the taste of his mother still in his mouth

and I knew it when she said *flowering caper bush*

the horses will eat grain until their stomachs explode:
guts on fetlocks and hocks. The smell of shit,

II.
of lime and ammonia, and then sawdust

asking, with darkness below the asking

cover the body with salt then prepare one hundred yards
of pure linen, inscribed with charms

like Napoleon's fertilizer enriched with mummies
like the gift of embalming spices—frankincense and myrrh

opening and closing her body,
stained fingertips pull solutions out of it—

a last meal of grain and meat,
simple blue tattoos on her hands, and a pattern of genes flow
between ancient delta populations

and then we doused ourselves in everclear,
lit ourselves on fire, and jumped into the lake.

III.
leaving only the heart in place—they believed it to be
the center of intelligence

while rubbing the crushed man's free arm,
I also administered the sedative

Patients in your letter

Day One: The boy hunting bobcats from a Plymouth; the lockjaw in the front row; seahorse-shaped babies pinching off.

Day Two: An unhappy suckling with brined hands; the conductor fell off a box as if he'd suddenly remembered.

Day Three: A man gone dead humping jungles; the opulence of some women.

Day Four: A cut of fat; hunching to blot the willing belly.

Day Five: Snow-blue lips; the spill of a mouthful of veins; a sloop in the bubble of uterine fervor.

Day Six: The girl drowned clubbing fishes in the curtsy of the sea; a cracked man in his father's warm paw.

Day Seven: The blemish of gooseflesh on her cognac-pink sex.

a dressing-down. a talking-to. the once-over clean-breast of it.

we, meaning everyone i've ever been involved with. *us*, specifically. who

i'm speaking with at this moment. suffering asking someone
to be kind to you. someone to forgive you for having ever lived without them,
   then rubbing

your last life all over them. collaboratively, it seems, we're pirating the benign
   experience.
i say it's not true but it is—up until the last moment, i hope
something will save me from disappointing you. contrite,

with some readiness. as they say, you can never forgive those first lovers.
how they make wrecks of it. how they're werewolves perched, then nestling—
wishing you'd been there.   everyone asked about you. everyone wishes

you'd budge. time sees us, but you knew that. interestingly enough.

How we separate

The slowness in things,
how they recur—

to walk together and not touch.
To salvage night.

Your one finger hooked
inside me
while you come. I cannot keep

from saying but I'll give up
my body—

let morning sink in
without touching.

I beg you to guess.
You keep guessing.

Blue-Norther

— after Roy V. Alleman

Barren cull cows
on the winter range. Milk cow and bull
rubbed down with a gunnysack in the shed.

The fenceline below snow. Sheep crawl
into snowbanks for warmth. Half of a face
swollen from freezing.

*

Rubbing snow on the face to ease the pain.
Waterblisters on wrists. A wool blanket,

a fur coat. Molasses cough drops
and snow for food. The greased wheels of the hayrack
buried until spring.

The blizzard blows a bare spot for the crippled cows.
Eyes frozen shut, chunks of ice the size
of quart jugs hang from their noses.

*

Harriet Bloom, a hundred year old
former slave, opens the door of her home
to watch the storm. Unable to close it,
she freezes in the doorway.

The foaming sides of her horse
harden when it stops to rest. Her bull sterile
from frozen testicles. Her son
over snowbanks on foot.

*

Lashed to the plane with ropes
he shoves bales out with his feet. A traveling man

breaks ice on water tanks. The haystacks
are like eggs in a great saucer. Drifting snow
scours hair off the rumps, and coyotes
tear at frozen hides.

*

Still sheep straddle fences.
Milk cows scattered
on the laketop. A cowman

slices holes through flanks to relieve
the bloat. On Bad Creek,
one cow in the top of a plum tree.

*

Two engines, a ballast car,
and a snowplow to dig out the tracks.
Hot coffee at the mortuary. Toboggans
pulled by halftracks.

The flying boxcar drops milk and mail.
A woman ties herself to the fencepost,
her dog in her shirt for warmth,

while her husband digs down into the snow
with a can of oil for the windmill.
No Flesh Canyon locked with snow.

Sally, a hard-mouthed horse; an unbroken
gelding named Fog who kicks and breaks fingers;
the palomino stallion; and a green mare named Topsy.

The brittle mane and tail of Fog blown off.
The mare runs through the four-wire fence
and falls into the slush-filled canyon. There she breaks
her neck, or drowns.

Halters rubbed off on the fence post. A cowman
to give up his horse and walk. How many
under drifts. Stabbing with the crowbar
hoping to strike a calf.

*

Dumping milk in the snow. I thought you were
my son. Swabbing the preacher's limbs
with kerosene to relieve the pain.

Packing the feet in snow. As they thaw, blood turns
the ice pink. His boots lost

stamping fire when the furnace exploded,
its flue packed with more snow.

He saw one steed caught up in the telephone wire
twenty feet above ground. His hog house
under, all the fat hogs dead.
Cattle walking over fences on snow.

*

Rendering trucks arrive to pull
the dead off the lake. The ears and tails
are gathered and fried. Some milk saved,
but the lantern kicked.

Living calves found by steam rising
from piles of snow. Untangling hooves
from fences. Cottonseed cakes donated
by Alabama for feed.

A woman trapped in her house
with the body of her son. The legs
of ranchers frozen off, the arm
of a wife.

*

The train rams snowdrifts.
The shed packed with snow,
backs of pigs rubbing the roof.

One calf stands by its frozen mother.
The rancher's children bat ice balls
from the noses of cows.

The Hunters

Last summer he turned over fields
for beans. The beans rose in straight lines.

The man rolls the bullet
between thumb and forefinger,

walks with a dog whose tumored
jaw was cut off. Whose tongue
drags in the snow.

That morning he'd dreamed
of his mother's miscarriage,
of swimming to a whale

frozen upside-down near his boat.

Young people cross a field of grass.

He's the same man driving the laundry truck;
his brother works night-shift at the donut shop.

There is also a woman
who wants to change her hair,

change everything. None
of them trust anyone.

They are on a trip
to see their old windows. White saltboxes

close together on a hill,
and earlier, one white house in the country.

She looks through that bathroom window
to remember her cigarette in the bathtub,

and the smell of oil from the basement.
There is a click at the window, it's her son.

He's been thinking in the snow, sees
shit rising up from it. He wants

to tell her the septic tank is overflowing.
He looks through the window, sees his sister,
a stream of red into the water.

His mother blows

a stream of smoke
to one nipple, and then the other.

January

Here. I knew it was going to save me.

This watery loop—snow-year,
        and the rocky shore. Birds feed
        so the cat in the window

can watch. To get the cat
        to believe. Water in the form of snow—

shroud of the dead year.
        Little strips from the girl's mouth.

It takes a long time: neat hands
        in a ceremony, seeds. Wasp eggs
        in the bird-skin. In the bougainvillea

and the bush. She thinks
        a cat drowned is better than a cat
        on fire. Wild cattle hump the dairy cows.

They plant the New Year Babies,
        and train cow-night to whiteness.

Surly Piggies

Luckily-cripplingly— let's highlight my well-being
for a moment: this little self-actualized life-long friend.

This pretty baby unicorn

tucks me in. This shabby workhorse
breaks a promise.   This little workforce waits for father's wink–it *is* a penance–

this *hankered after* pays its own way.
This little potency   shares as much benevolence with the world
as she can. This "No-Fault" divorce
unites my theory

with practice.   For partnerships out of love's reach. This little prophecy–what the New
Masculinity should flush: this, strictly speaking,   *wee wee wee*

through the church-contest.   To the junctures of my meta-
tarsals   (I jokingly call "the wimps"). Or, my brave little

uprights.

Steak/Pork

1.
The water as bright as snow
in the dark. Water's

blackness. It is very late.
It's a bad day, as you are today— a rock

the size of a bedroom beneath the washed
mountain. Light-ball
that catches the light, ruins the dress.

Winter, pin-prick. Chickens,
you say, are idiots—

washed for ruin. Night legs.

You say I am not careful.
I can't be more

specific. Two, or three times,
to whores

who called to my legs.
Who say I'm free to pig.

That the pig reads.

That the pig's a new settlement: untouched,

tracing you in moving darkness. Like feeling
with fingers you can't find.

Your bits of paper
for hours. How to say it without

saying *a familiar snow.*

2.
If you can live,
then I can live. South Pole pigs, you tell me,
eat. Have disappeared between houses.

You, on the white screen one night. You,

on the moon-
viewing bridge.

Trees have been witness

from pine to piñon. Caterpillar's hair—
plus anticipation. The feeling is:

a viewing, and the whole thing missed.
People already know about faith

and the end of privacy; the hidden
ways of each.

I always knew the two pleasures: the tree away from tree,
and old elegances, one by one

spared. Only two things can happen.
What is my question?

Why pigeons are awkward

from the tar, then cleaned in begging position. Wanting,

and not wanting attention. Too public
a bird-revelation. People forget omissions. Are you ever
released again? Maybe that is the question.

It's also less than that. Flea-

bite on the snail. Nerve behind
the iris. Accumulate

to uncover. Cover, to reveal. And the ones
left unrevealed? Possibly, the dummy fire.

Horse-Boat

there can only be intelligence
in all of Iceland's bees—

the beehive huts, wild ponies
with long hair

who sleep
where there are only stones.
Stir, and stir—

the horse-boat and houses
cut from stone for warmth.
The yellow-topped

heads of girls in a field

who could not judge correctly
the distances the mountains.
No longer thinking

as in a plain. All the darling
skins of animals—

the stack of flattened cheetahs,
the flat bird-body

of the unshelled tortoise
force-fed an orange

before death. Brother king

and sister queen
yell *Hawaii*, you give them

their Halloween candy. In cradles
where we stick together

I'll not want anything
you have—your mediocre

communion, which is not technical.
But too much

finished—
you are complicated enough

as you are.
Remember when the snow

took us? When the boat
turned, and we slept.

Prophecy Spots

Deer appear at the edges.
Our dog is burning, so you cut off
her legs.

She dances madly in the field
while I am alone with her murderer. I nod
and nod. The ice complains all night.

You say everyone is apart
from at least one child. One that we were
or one that we want. And the day
gives in and gives in.

Falling twin stars open their hands,
stumble into some building.
Perhaps, Night,
you didn't need them anymore?

Or let me put it this way:
the moon awakens with empty hands,
her legs rattle.